THE 50'S PLUS:
TO WORK OR
NOT TO WORK

THE 50'S PLUS: TO WORK OR NOT TO WORK

◆

An opportunity to examine your future work options

Mary Ann Peters

iUniverse, Inc.
New York Lincoln Shanghai

THE 50'S PLUS: TO WORK OR NOT TO WORK
An opportunity to examine your future work options

iUniverse books may be ordered through booksellers or by contacting:

iUniverse
2021 Pine Lake Road, Suite 100
Lincoln, NE 68512
www.iuniverse.com
1-800-Authors (1-800-288-4677)

ISBN-13: 978-0-595-38737-3 (pbk)
ISBN-13: 978-0-595-83119-7 (ebk)
ISBN-10: 0-595-38737-3 (pbk)
ISBN-10: 0-595-83119-2 (ebk)

Printed in the United States of America

Contents

This chapter will examine the pluses and minuses involved in remaining in your current job. It will also address the possibility of promotion if a choice is made to stay. The content will cover facets of the values connected with the reasons you choose to stay in your current position.

This chapter will outline useful information on how to find other opportunities available within your current company. It will provide hints on the "internal job search", such as networking, dealing with your current management personnel, and interacting with Human Resources Staff.

This chapter will give useful information on how to put together a resume, how to answer posted ads, how to network, and how to use recruiters.

This chapter will look at the pros and cons of accepting an early retirement package. It will address not only financial issues, but, more importantly, what will you do to keep yourself occupied both mentally and physically.

This chapter will explore the idea of working part time or becoming a consultant within your current company or outside of your current company. It will explore various options of the term part time/consulting.

This chapter will talk about a few alternatives that may be options for the person who chooses to own their own business (franchising/buying an existing company/ or beginning a new start-up company.)

This chapter will pull together a lot of questions that are part of retirement: leisure, volunteering, use of skills, family concerns, geographic preferences, etc.

This chapter will discuss the types of considerations you may want to undertake, especially if you choose to "take some time off" while pursuing options outside of your current company.

This chapter will allow you to think about the options of pursuing an undergraduate or graduate degree as well as pursuing continuing education during your work or retirement life.

This chapter will allow you time to explore the many areas in which you may wish to share your knowledge either through formal settings (universities/colleges) or informal settings (workplace, community outreach, etc.)

This short chapter will allow you to develop a realistic timeline to implement your decisions.

INTRODUCTION

✦

Welcome to the 50's/60's Arena of Life

This book will give you an opportunity to reflect on your Career/Work Life…where you have been, where you are, and where you hope to be during the remainder of your work life. You will accomplish this through the reading of written essays and through short exercises designed to help you reflect on the content of the written exercises. This book is intended to aid you in determining the various options available to the 50's/60's age group in the career/work segment of life. Remember, this time in life can become a time of excitement—of newness-or a time of concern in many facets of personal, social, family, and career arenas. You have had a considerable amount of experience thus far and are able to reflect on these experiences and how they have shaped your life up to this present time, and how they will shape the remainder of your lived life. And this time in your life is an ideal time to take notice of and plan for your future work/career life. Hopefully, these materials will entice you to reflect on the many issues facing you as you move into the "pre-retirement" or retirement phase of your work life.

This book can be used by individuals or in a group/seminar setting.

ACKNOWLEDGEMENTS

This book was written with the advice and help of many personal and professional colleagues. In particular I am grateful to:

*Dr. Constance J. Pritchard who has been instrumental as a mentor and friend

*My Changes and Challenges Support Group

*My many professional colleagues over the years

*My good friend, Jane Wilwerding

*My supportive family members: Tom, Nanci, Dick, Pat, Bob

*The staff at iUniverse who have coached me throughout the publishing process

They have all been a source of encouragement throughout this process.

1

SHOULD YOU STAY IN YOUR PRESENT JOB?

On first take, it would seem that the logical decision is not to "rock the boat." From all accounts the job market may be somewhat stagnant and you may feel that it is better to leave well enough alone. But, you may also choose to take a look at your present situation and analyze all the factors on "staying/leaving" before you make a final decision.

In making a decision to stay in your present job, a number of questions need to be examined:

1.   Do you enjoy going to work on a daily basis? There is something to be said for the person who is able to enjoy going to work. You look forward to your days off, but the aspects that are a part of your current job also energize you. With this question, the key becomes "enjoyment on a regular basis", not answering this question in a negative vein because of a bad day or a sporadic time of non-enjoyment. You may also want to check if you are "feeling" physically good, when you go into work. If the workplace or the job is a source of stress, you may need to reevaluate why you are staying put in your place of work.

2.   Are your skills being used continually in your current job? The use of your talents and skills is extremely important. If you are using your innate or learned skills consistently, you will be energized, and this

energy will carry over into your personal life. Not using skills on a regular basis can be a source of de-energy. And when you take a look at your skills, are you enjoying the skills that you are using? It is one thing to be good at doing things, but it is quite another to enjoy using those skills.

3.   Are you proud of the work you do? This question can also be looked at with another question, "when people ask you what you do, can you answer them directly or are you hedging because you are not feeling excited about your job description or your responsibilities? While, it may be trite, most people do ask you about your job and what you do. It seems to be a starting point for conversation. You want to look and sound excited when you talk about your career/your job. You don't want to offer excuses for what you do.

4.   Are you choosing to remain in your job because of the benefits and pension? If the answer is affirmative, and you enjoy your work, then the reason for remaining is productive. Benefits and pension give you a sense of security for the future, and this security may be enough of a cause to remain in your current position. However, you may need to check out if the security is real. Many times companies make choices to downsize long-term employees. And also, in today's environment, there are companies that are no longer offering pensions. So, be sure, if you answer affirmative, that the pensions are for real and that you won't be disappointed if you stay and the pension is removed.

5.   Is there an opportunity for promotion if you remain in your current position? Sometimes, you may choose to remain in a position because of the room for advancement. If this is a possibility, you may choose to remain in your current job at this point in your life, since it gives you an opportunity for career growth without leaving your present company. But, it is important to utilize your skills if you get

promoted. Will your best skill set be used in a new/higher level position? If promotion is a strong possibility for you then you may choose to stay where you are at this point.

6.   Do you like to have a job that is close to home? You do not have to fight traffic on a daily basis. Therefore, you can spend more time at home versus traveling and this is important to you at this point in your life. Or on the other hand, if your job is further away from home you may choose to stay in the position, because it gives you the down time to relax as you drive to and from work.

7.   Are your work values being met in your current position? Some of these values may be: ethics/relationships with team members/security/ being able to be self-actualized/chance for advancement/family responsibilities/chance to travel/etc. Whatever is important to you, at this point in your life, needs to be a part of why you choose to remain in your current position.

As long as you are honest with yourself on why you choose to remain in your current job and you are comfortable with this choice—then to remain is an option. However, it is always important to take time to occasionally reflect on why you are staying in your current position. If the answers prove to be somewhat negative you may decide it is time to explore other options.

TEST

Do you enjoy going to work?	YES	NO
Are you using your skills?	YES	NO
What are some of these skills?		
Are you proud of your work?	YES	NO
Are your benefits and pension keeping you in your current job?	YES	NO
Is there an opportunity for promotion in your present job?	YES	NO
What work values are helping you choose to stay in your current job?		
Do you enjoy working with the current persons in your work group?	YES	NO
Are you comfortable in working with your current management?	YES	NO
Are you beginning to feel burned out in your present job?	YES	NO
Is your current job in line with your personality type?	YES	NO
Do you have to take a lot of work home with you?	YES	NO

2

SHOULD YOU LOOK FOR ANOTHER OPPORTUNITY IN YOUR CURRENT COMPANY?

In order for the above option to be a viable choice for you, there may be a number of positive factors that serve as concrete reasons to wanting to stay in your current company, but in a different position. Among these factors are:

*Your current company has a pension and a set of benefits that give you a sense of security for the future, especially for your future retirement. This benefit along with other sources of income provided by your company is important to you as you plan for the next phase of your work life.

*There are other opportunities within your current company that would give you a chance to use your skills and experiences. A movement to another position within the company does not always include a monetary raise, but many times, as you mature, the money becomes less important, as long as the security facets are taken care of. Plus, sometimes, a change of scenery can be a source of new energy for you.

*Changes and internal transfers are encouraged within the company. And this becomes and important factor. You don't want to make a change, if the company is not behind you 100%. You want to be able to realize support in your choice.

*Taking a new position within the company would reenergize you. This reason is tied to the first option. Many times, the reason you do not have a "Monday Morning Smile" when you go to work, is not because you find the "company" frustrating, but you may be burned out in performing your present job responsibilities.

*Loyalty to your present company is very important to you. And this is a very noble value. Be sure, that the loyalty is both ways, and that the company is also wanting and willing to have you stay with them.

*If you stay within your present company, the chances of your being downsized are very minimal. This is a bit hard to concretize. The best barometer is to notice if there are a lot of changes happening within the company, or if downsizing has already become part of the program.

*Taking a new position with the company would not jeopardize your work values. Again, this goes back to being sure that you are doing this move for the right reason.

*You would be able to take a new position within the company and give it your all, not just take it to live out your years until retirement. You want to be careful of this reason. If you do not really want to give a new opportunity 100% of your energy, you need to be careful. Your work performance could suffer in a new position, due to lack of interest, and this in turn could result in a termination.

*You would enjoy working with a new group of colleagues and managers. This does not mean that you do not enjoy your current team members, but sometimes being with new people can be a source of new thinking for you also.

The above represent a few of the conditions that may be present when choosing to move to another position within the company. As long as you make a conscious decision to explore other opportunities and are aware of your motivations, it may be the ideal time for you to explore the ramifications of this decision.

If you decide to do this, there are a number of action steps you need to undertake in order to make the move.

1.   Explore other areas of interest within the company. This can be done by requesting job descriptions from Human Resources, talking with people who currently are doing the jobs of interest, and networking with others outside of the company who currently do the type of work in which you are interested. As you talk with these people, be sure you let them know that you are exploring ideas, only. You may find out that some areas that seemed interesting may not be right for you.

2.   Talk with your current manager and let them know your thoughts and the reasons you wish to make change. Ask for their support, both in letting you move and in letting you contact future management to talk about your wishes. Remind them that you are only in the exploration stage. Management personnel can be excellent sources of referral for you, if you eventually make a decision to move to a new area. You want your manager on your side.

3.   Talk with a representative in the Human Resources Department to find out how to move to another area of the company. You may want to ask them if they offer any career advising to be sure you are heading in the right direction. Once again, the personnel in Human Resources may appreciate you asking them for advice and help.

Moving to a new position within your current company may be just the tonic needed to give new meaning to your work, while at the same time allowing for continued security and benefits.

SELF TEST

*What are some of the jobs of interest to you in your current company?

*Staying within your present company is important for the following reasons:

Money...how much do you need?

Vacation...how much time do you need?

Health Insurance...how long will you need it?

Management style...you know that the current group of management cares for its employees.

Ethics...the company has been and continues to operate "above board."

Location...the company is within reasonable distance for you.

Teamwork...other people in the company would like you to work for them.

(If you decide to remain in your current company, you need to make some of the following plans)

*You will meet with your manager, by this date.

*You will meet with your current manager and talk with them about your plans by this date.

*You will talk with someone in Human Resources by this date.

3

SHOULD YOU LEAVE YOUR CURRENT JOB AND YOUR CURRENT COMPANY?

Once you have made a decision to leave your current job/company there are a number of practical steps you need to undertake in searching for a new opportunity.

1. Come to a decision on what it is you want to do or which company you wish to work for. There are a few ideas to help you undertake this activity:

*Research companies that may be of interest to you. This can be done through a variety of sources, the local Business Journal, the Book of Lists, Internet databases and websites that contain the annual reports of companies.

*Scan the help wanted ads and get an idea of companies that may be in a hiring mode. It also gives you an opportunity to find out what types of jobs and skills are being advertised. While this may prove to be a daunting task, this exercise can lead to you researching more information about the companies that are currently advertising for clients, or, if you see the same company continually advertising for identical positions week after week, it may send up a red flag for you.

*Relook at your experience and skill set to determine if there is a match for jobs you determine are pertinent for you. Make note of those companies and those jobs so you can prepare to send them the needed materials that they require.

*Research job descriptions on the Internet to identify responsibilities and skills needed for certain positions. This is particularly helpful if you think something is interesting, but you have no idea just what the responsibilities entail.

2. *Prepare an updated resume.*

*Go to the library or find sources on the Internet that provide tools on how to write a good resume. Choose a style that gives you an opportunity to not only explain your work history but also your accomplishments.

*Take into account your skills as you put together your resume. Many times it is the skills that you can transfer to a new job or company, not necessarily just your experience.

*Engage the services of a professional resume writer to aid you in writing your document.

3. *Begin the process of networking with people to let them know of your decision to leave your current company.*

*Compose a listing of people that you will talk with regarding your decision to change jobs and companies. These people can be family members, colleagues at work, professional colleagues, neighbors, relatives, and a host of other people.

*Set a time when you will meet with these contacts. These times should be uninterrupted times (not during the family reunion). Let them know you are not asking for a job, but want to get their input as you explore your decision. (Remember, people are always willing to give advice.)

4. Prepare a listing of items for discussion with these contacts.

*Let them know that you are exploring other areas of interest and that you want to "pick their brain" as you begin this process.

*Ask them questions about what they like or dislike about their job or company.

*Ask questions about what types of skills are needed in their company or profession.

*Tell them your skills and find out if they are applicable to their company.

*Lastly, ask them if they have contacts you could meet with to discuss your career choices.

The interesting thing about networking is that the person with whom you are interacting should be talking 80% of the time, and you only 20% of the time. You want their advice. Too, often, in the past, networking meant interacting with people to find a job. This type of networking is a source of research for you.

5. Contact recruiters that may be of help in your job change, especially if you wish to remain in the same field.

*Obtain a listing of recruiters using the Yellow Pages or the Kennedy Directory of Recruiters.

*Send a cover letter enlisting their help in your job search. Let them know of your skills and few selected accomplishments. Also inform them of your salary and geographic preferences. This can be done via e-mail.

6. Answer ads that are of interest you. These ads may be on the net, in the newspapers, in professional publications, or in college alumni publications.

*Write a cover letter in response to the ad.

*Attach a copy of your prepared resume.

*Respond to the ad in the manner requested by the company. This may be filling out an application on line.

7. Engage the services of a professional career advisor to help you in your decision to change jobs and companies. These meetings can become a source of personal growth and reflection for you, which can be very important as you reach the 50's Plus.

*The professional will help you make decisions based on your values, skills, goals, and experiences.

*The professional will help you explore a variety of possibilities.

*The professional will help you be realistic about your future options.

*The professional will guide you through the "change" process.

Once you have made a decision to leave your current company and your current job, the process of looking for something new can become very invigorating. If your current situation is somewhat frustrating for you, this new venture of exploring other options outside of your company can be a source of newness and renewal.

SELF TEST

*Make a listing of companies of interest to you.

*Prepare a list of possible networking contact to utilize in your search.

*Prepare a draft of your resume.

*Prepare a list of items to discuss with your contacts.

*Find five jobs in the paper or on the net that you wish to apply for and send in the applications.

4

SHOULD YOU TAKE AN EARLY RETIREMENT PACKAGE?

This question can be considered both a blessing and a frustration. If you have been planning all along to take an early retirement package, if offered, it will be a blessing question. If you had been hoping to work at this company for some more time and all of a sudden are faced with this situation, it can be a frustration question.

1. Among the considerations for taking an early retirement package are the following:

*The package will act as a cushion, both from the financial and benefits arena, until a pension or social security becomes active.

*A package will give some financial peace while looking for another job.

*An early retirement package can become an extra nest egg that can be used for the future, while employed in a new job.

*An early "out" package can give opportunities to have enough security to do some of the volunteer or part time work that you always wanted to do.

*An early retirement package may give you the additional monies that you have always wanted to use to begin your own business venture.

*An early out package may be just what you needed to explore other ventures in your work life. You no longer can stay "put" and be complacent.

2. Among the concerns that come with an early retirement package are the following:

*If you take the first package offered, there may be a better package offered in the future. In this case you may want to wait, but then there is the concern, if you wait will the new package be better than the one currently being offered.

*If you have not made any plans concerning this reality, anger may set in. You begin to question why me and not someone else. And if this happens, the excitement of using an early out package quickly subsides.

3. An early retirement package can bring about a myriad of concerns regarding what you will do if you are not working.

If you need to continue to work, for awhile, there my be concerns such as:

*You think you are too old to be employed somewhere else. And this is a special concern for the 50's Plus age group. This is not always realistic, but it is a concern.

*You don't know any job except this one. And this is a real issue. You need to reanalyze your skills and use this as an opportunity for change. You will be amazed.

*You don't have very much money to live on. This could be a serious concern. You may need to take a temporary job to bring in some additional cash, while you are looking for the right opportunity.

*You may be concerned, that if other potential employees offer you a job, and they realize you took an early retirement package, they may choose to undercut your salary, thinking that you have a "cache" of cash to live on.

4. Most of the time, when a person is offered an early retirement package, there are signs that lead up to this offering. It becomes important to realize these signs early on, so that you can make adequate preparations.

*The company is being sold to another corporation.

*The company is steadily losing sales and money

*The company is already offering "buy-outs" to individuals.

*The company is part of an industry that is obsolete.

Early retirement packages have become a daily occurrence in today's economy. No company is shielded form this reality. And therefore, if companies are always in this state of flux, it behooves you, as an employee, to be proactive in thinking through the realities connected with this reality. And one word of caution, if you receive a buy out package and are not ready to retire, either financially or personally, do not use the monies given and waste them and your time to begin something new. Too often, the monies may give out sooner than expected, or your sense of self worth may give out, also. You want to take the severance and be proactive in how you approach this time in life.

SELF TEST

*What are some of the jobs you could do if you took an early retirement package?

*If you received an early retirement plan, what would you do with the buy out monies?

*What benefits will you need that are not covered by the early retirement plan?

*What are your financial needs for the next year? The next five years?

*If offered the opportunity, what would it take to volunteer to take the buy out package?

*If needing to continue to work, how long can you live on the buy-out monies?

*How much time, if you need to continue to work, will you take off before looking for a new opportunity?

*Do you know any friends who took an early retirement package? What can you learn from them?

5

SHOULD YOU WORK AS A CONSULTANT OR A PART TIME EMPLOYEE?

Once you have made the decision to be no longer employed as a full time employee, either in your present company or in a new environment, an opportunity presents itself to explore other options if you wish to continue to utilize your skills and experiences.

PART TIME WORK

You may want to work part time at your current company. This option will give you:

1. an opportunity to stay in a known environment

2. an opportunity to continue using your skills.

3. an opportunity to maintain some of your benefits.

4. an opportunity to continue a mitigated stream of income.

5. an opportunity to arrange your own work schedule, since being in a familiar environment, management is more willing to arrange a win-win schedule with someone with whom they are familiar.

As you make a decision to stay in your current work place on a part time basis, take the necessary steps required by your company to move from a full time to a part time position. That may include talking with your present management person and with staff in the Human Resources Department. It may be possible to stay in your current position or you may need to move into a new area of the company that is willing to work with you to meet your requirements to work on a part time basis.

You may wish to work on a part time basis in an environment outside of your current company. This could include working for an organization that is completely new to your experience. (ie: selling clothing for major department store/setting up a home office to telemarket products/editing books for a publishing company/etc.). Or it may be in an organization with whom you are familiar, and a place that would welcome hiring you with a known skill set that you have already utilized.

If you choose the option of part time employment, and are currently in the Social Security Program, be sure you check with the Social Security Agency to understand any ramifications that may impact your income status. There are tax ramifications, if you choose to take Social Security before the full benefit age time is in effect.

CONSULTING WORK

This is a wonderful opportunity for you to utilize both your skills and your experience. There are several ways in which you can move into a consulting business.

*The first way is to talk with your current management about the possibility of moving from full time work into consulting work within your present department or company. This could be a win-win situation for you and the company. The benefits for you would be:

1. you would be able to work on an as needed basis in a known environment

2. you would be able to negotiate an hourly or project fee for your services

3. you could negotiate your time schedule.

4. you could become an "expert" in a very specific needed area.

The benefits for the company would be:

1. they could use your experience

2. they would not be responsible for the benefit portion of the compensation

3. they would work with a known person, who does not need "training time."

*The second way to work as a consultant is to establish your own consulting business where you can work for many organizations. This option would give you an opportunity to zero in on the utilization of your expertise to influence many types of projects. To do individual consulting demands a variety of actions.

1. researching the marketplace to determine organizations which could benefit from your services.

2. establishing your own business operations, which would emphasize a specific area of expertise.

3. marketing your services to businesses.

4. establishing a pricing schedule.

5. performing the work proficiently and productively to establish network referrals.

This option can be fulfilling both in terms of income and recognition, (but it can also be frustrating, if contracts do not come your way.)

*The third way is to join an existing consulting firm in your area. You can search for this information in the Yellow Pages, the Book of Lists, Internet Sources, etc. The process for joining an existing firm is the same as "searching for a job." It demands networking with people who can lead you to a possible hiring.

Working part time or as a consultant can be a rewarding experience. Either option needs to be explored in terms of time, income, availability and utilization of skills.

SELF TEST

Do you want to work part time?   YES NO

If yes, list the work that you would like to do in your present company.

OR

If yes, list the work that you would like to do for another organization.

Do you want to be a consultant?   YES NO

If yes, what type of consulting would you do in your present company?

OR

If yes, what type of consulting firm do you wish to join? List names.

OR

If yes, what steps do you need to take to begin your own consulting firm?

6

SHOULD YOU OWN YOUR OWN BUSINESS

In today's economy, there are many new "cottage" industries springing up. As you get downsized, or as you look for ways to "do what you always wanted to do", the possibility of starting your own business becomes very attractive. Basically, there are three alternatives that are available to you as you pursue this dream.

Buy an existing company (independence and autonomy).

This alternative presumes that you have available finances, either personally or through investors.

Before beginning the process of buying an existing company, choose an industry or company that is of interest to you. There may be a lot of good "buys" out there, but they need to be in conjunction with your interests, skills, and experiences. Otherwise, you will not be able to give it your all, since you are not fully engaged in the outcomes of the products or services.

A good way to find out about companies that may be looking for potential buyers is to talk with lawyers or bankers. They may be in contact with companies that may have owners who wish to retire from owning a business or they may know of owners who wish to sell due to financial reasons. another source of information is to talk with persons in the Venture Capital Industry. This group of individuals may be able to help you with cash investments, and it can be a win-win for them and for you.

Once, you decide to buy a company, it is important that you take time to study, in depth, the financials of the organization, the past, present, and projected growth of the company, and the existing personnel in the company. This "due diligence" will give you the necessary tools to make an informed decision. You can do this by asking for all the financials and either evaluate it yourself or engage the services of a lawyer/tax person to aid you in the "due diligence. You should also talk with the existing personnel on a confidential basis to get their input about the "real realities" of the company.

Once the purchase is made, the real work begins. You will need to put into place an exceptional management team composed of existing or new personnel who are in agreement with your vision and your goals. You will need to delegate the day-to-day working responsibilities, so you can concentrate on the "big picture." You will also, need to put around you a trusted group of individuals who will be honest with you as you solicit their opinions.

Buy a Franchised Business (independence without autonomy).

This alternative presumes you have the finances available to buy into the franchise; most of the franchises let you know the upfront costs.

This option has the rewards of owning a company, yet having available resources for the actual operations of the business. There are professionals available to help you find the right franchises to operate.

They will help you find the perfect fit that meets your interests and your finances, along with your career goals.

Certain types of franchises offer marketing, operational, and financial help for you on a regular basis. You use their system to run a very effective business. On the other hand, there are franchises or licensees that allow you to use our own creativity in marketing, finances, and operations. They give some corporate help, but you are able to use their known name for a determined fee.

Begin a New Business from Scratch (autonomy and independence).

This alternative, once again, presumes you have the necessary start-up monies. Interestingly, these beginning monies may not be as costly, since most startup ventures are smaller in size, therefore, less in costs and overhead. (This alternative could be undertaken by you alone, or with some partners.)

This alternative will give you the excitement of owning and directing your own business; from inception to operation, to fulfillment. It may be very small and niche oriented (usually a service venture.)

It is necessary, that your own business, begun from the ground up be cemented with a well-defined business plan outlining your mission, goals, financials, marketing, etc. A good source to aid you in writing such a plan is the Internet, local banks, or the Small Business Loan Agency.

This alternative can be very rewarding; yet can be very time consuming. The idea is to remain with your goal and not give up in the hard times. The end can justify the tasks it takes to get there.

Whatever choice you take to "own your own business, the choice will give you a chance to fulfill your dream of independence, independence with both risks and opportunities.

SELF TEST

*What current business opportunities exist that you are willing to research and possibly buy?

*What type of monies do you have available to invest in a new business?

*What other individuals would you enlist to help you both financially and operationally?

*What franchise opportunities interest you?

*What is more important in choosing a franchise? (upfront monies/ type of business/marketing/location search/public name recognition/etc.)

*What type of small start up businesses interest you?

*Would you run the business by yourself or would you hire employees?

7

SHOULD YOU MAKE A DECISION TO RETIRE FULL TIME?

This question is quite different from the question about "should you take an early retirement package?" Usually, by the time you come to a retirement decision there are a number of factors already in place that make full time retirement an option. It is these factors that will be addressed in this chapter.

1. You have reached an age where you can begin to collect your social security benefits. This may be an age of taking early social security or an age whereby you can obtain the full social security benefit. In making this decision based on social security, it may be to your advantage to take early pay versus waiting until the full benefit is available. This is something you may wish to talk over with your tax advisor.

2. You have reached an age where you no longer have to worry about the medical benefits connected with company insurance. Usually, this comes about when you have a spouse who carries medical insurance, or you have reached a time in your life whereby Medicare will begin to pick up your medical benefits.

3. You have sufficient monies in your retirement savings, your pension, and your social security that you can live comfortably without having to constantly worry about money.

4. If in a relationship with another person, both of you agree that the time to retire is now. It may be that both parties are at the same point in their life and retirement benefits will be available to both, or it may be that one person will retire while the other person continues to work for medical or other benefits.

5. You have thought through the challenges that will come with retirement. Challenges such as:

> What will you do with your time?

> Are you ready to do volunteer service?

> If in a relationship, what new types of scheduling will you both have to make?

> Will you become involved in hobbies or projects?

> What will you do to keep your mind stimulated?

6. You look forward to the time of retirement. This is very important before you actually make a retirement decision. Having a plan, feeling excited about the future, and taking the necessary steps to exercise that new future can lead to excitement about retirement.

7. Your health is relatively good at this time, or there may be health issues that are starting to be a concern to you, and you realize that if you want to enjoy life to the fullest at this time in your life, it may be the time to retire and do the things you have always wanted to do. Sometimes, if you choose to wait, you may experience other health

issues and then you will become frustrated at yourself for not making a decision to retire—sooner.

8. You no longer want to worry about a schedule or about responsibilities. You want to take life as it comes, and work life is not letting this happen.

Full time retirement can become an exciting reality for you. Age wise, you reach a point when this opportunity presents itself to you. But in the end, it is not only age that enters into the decision; it is also your physical, psychological, and spiritual well-being.

SELF TEST

*From a financial standpoint, would it be better to take early social security benefits or wait until the full pay age?

*Will you be able to afford the medical insurance connected with early social security?

*Why types of supplement will you need once you reach Medicare insurance benefit age?

*What are your monthly needs in terms of finances?

*What monies do you need to save for future needs?

*What monies do you need for extra daily/monthly occasions?

*What will you do with your time once you retire?

8

SHOULD YOU TAKE A PAID SABBATICAL WHILE MAKING YOUR FUTURE DECISIONS?

It is a common occurrence, within the higher educational profession, to have time away from regular teaching duties to pursue additional coursework or experiences related to their teaching field. This time away is generally recognized as a "sabbatical."

A paid sabbatical is something that you may wish to take while trying to make an important decision about your future. This type of "time off" presumes adequate finances and the decision not to remain within your current job or you current company.

There are a number of reasons, why you may choose to take a "paid sabbatical" while making important future decisions, rather than just taking full time off from a job.

1. This in-between job can be a factor in personal productivity and self worth. Sometimes, when you are unemployed or between choices, your self-esteem can be affected, and while work is not the only factor in self worth undertaking, an in-

between full or part time job can help you feel better about yourself.

2. The "paid sabbatical" can give you additional experience in an area in which you wish to gain further knowledge and understanding. Not only will you be giving productive service to an employer during this time, but also you will be expanding your skill set to aid you in exploring other options.

3. The interim job may be a source of actual career choice. While you may think that the job will be only a paid sabbatical, it may turn out to be an unanticipated career choice for your 50's/60's future.

4. The "paid sabbatical" can give you a tremendous source of possibilities to meet new people. These people can then become a part of your networking group. Some of these new contacts may be managers, co-workers, vendors, clients, and others who may turn you on to some real choice possibility.

5. The "paid sabbatical" can help "pay the bills." It can bring in some additional income to ease any concerns that may creep into your decision making time.

Remember, the "paid sabbatical" is a time to bridge the gap between your former choice of job and a new choice of career/retirement. It can give you a time of financial security and a time of continued self-esteem.

SELF TEST

*If you are leaving your current place of employment, and want to make a decision for future choice, do you want to take a "paid sabbatical"?

*What type of "jobs" would interest you in terms of working during your time off period?

*Would you consider a full time or a part time "paid sabbatical?"

*Do you need additional finances while you are in the "future-thinking mode?

*How long would you see yourself in the "in between" job before you make your decision to move into the next phase?

9

SHOULD YOU PURSUE FURTHER EDUCATION

As you move along in your life span and reach the 50's 60's age group, you may wonder whether you should pursue some further education for a variety of reasons: to finish that first degree you never completed/ to take courses related to a career/job that would improve your edge in future employment/to undertake a master's or doctorate degree to give you more credibility in your current or newly chosen field.

<u>UNDERGRADUATE DEGREE</u>

Going back to school to complete a first degree can become a source of pride for you. You may constantly regret the fact that you never completed your education, or even began a college degree. As a result you may find yourself defensive when people bring up the topic of education, particularly the topic of a degree. And sometimes this source of regret can lead you to overemphasize your experience since you may want to "look good" to others.

If you choose to complete an undergraduate degree, for whatever reason—personal pride-credibility—overcome regret, there are some very creative options you need to look into and research. Many universities and colleges give the adult person the option to "count" some of their work experiences toward the fulfillment of a degree. This option can significantly reduce the amount of hours you need to expend in classroom study. You may also receive some credit for courses taken in the past or for continuing educational seminars that relate to your degree. While researching this topic, you also want to decide what type of degree and what type of scheduling will best fit into your situation. There are a variety of schedules available for the adult student: weekend only classes, once a week evening classes, on-line classes, large/small group seminars, intensive classes that meet for nine week periods. The choices are myriad.

It may behoove you to meet with a number of different college/university counselors to get a better idea of tuition costs, appropriate degree, creative scheduling opportunities, and length of time to complete the coursework.

Two interesting sidelines in choosing to go "back to school" is that you will be able to interact with new networking contacts. Plus, if you are in a company that offers tuition assistance, this may be a win-win situation for you.

GRADUATE DEGREE

If you decide to pursue a graduate degree, especially a degree within your chosen field of interest, you may find that this experience will give you a chance to really concentrate in an area of total interest to you. Your classes will consist of topics of real interest and not just topics you need to take to complete a program (as is sometimes the case in under-graduate study). The graduate study will also give you the opportunity to network with a niche group of people who may become the catalysts for you in your search for your future direction at this point in your life. Once again, the company for which you work may be willing to pay for your courses, courses that are generally designed for you as an adult student. Time, scheduling, on-line programs are readily available through most universities.

CONTINUING EDUCATION

This topic is realities for the 50's/60's person, whether you choose to stay where you are, move to a new company, consult, or retire. In this day and age, the only "constant is change" and in order for you to take command of change, you need to be educated to the changes happening around you.

The types of continuing education are myriad: community college courses, CEU seminars in a field that requires a certain updating annually, conventions, self study courses, business related seminars, alumni association meetings, technical meetings/seminars, etc.

Some of these educational experiences may be directly related to your current work, some of them may be related to a career that you intend to pursue, some of them may be centered on topics related to retirement, and some of them may be for personal development (which will help you in all relational interactions).

As you can observe, continuing education, degreed or non-degreed oriented will definitely be a source of growth in your future years and may be a source of "new life" if you choose to remain in the workforce in some capacity.

SELF TEST

*Do you plan to finish an undergraduate degree?

*After research, from which university will you complete your degree?

*For what purpose do you want to complete an undergraduate degree?

*Do you plan to pursue or finish a graduate degree?

*In what field of interest will you pursue a graduate degree?

*For what purpose will you pursue a graduate degree?

*What are some of the continuing educational experiences that you will undertake in the next few months?

*Will theses experiences be related to work, to retirement, or to personal growth?

10

SHOULD YOU USE YOUR EXPERIENCES TO BECOME A TEACHER?

This question becomes a very real question as you enter the 50's/60's phase of your life.

You have had a considerable amount of lived work experience. You have had the opportunity to utilize your skill set and to develop new skills. You have had to learn to cope with various workplace situations (from the very good to the very trying). You have copious technical knowledge both from the textbook and from true and tried operations.

You have learned how manage projects. You have learned how to lead people. In reality, you are a bundle of knowledge, knowledge that you may want to pass on to the future workforce.

Fortified with all of the above realities how do you go about sharing this knowledge, either in a structured or non-structured environment.

*You may want to teach at a University or College. In order to do this, you will need to approach the Academic Leader of the Institution to learn the processes you need to undertake to begin this new venture.

This may involve writing a "curriculum vitae" (the educational term for resume). It may necessitate that you have earned a Master's Degree in the field in which you wish to teach. In some instances it may require that you have a Doctorate Degree.

If you decide to pursue this route and begin to instruct students, you will discover the joy of being the facilitator of knowledge—the expert in your field. And your students will believe what you say, since you have actually lived the message, not just passed on textbook knowledge.

*You may want to use your technical knowledge to teach courses in a Community College or Technical School environment. Once again, you will need to become acquainted with the protocol on how to become an instructor in one of these organizations. In some instances, especially in the Technical Colleges, your hands on experience combined with your "book knowledge" are extremely important. You will actually teach not only text knowledge, but will work with the students in "lab" situations whereby, you can judge whether your spoken word is being actualized in real experiences.

*You may want to become a "trainer" within your own company or organization. Many times these training experiences are coordinated through the Human Resources or Training Department. You can approach them to express your desire to pass on knowledge in formal classes to other employees in the company.

*You may offer your services to become the "in house" expert within your department in your current company. As new employees enter your area of work, they often need to have expert training on topics related to work processes, procedures, etc. Many times the Management personnel do not have the adequate time to train the new staff members. You could become the "Departmental Trainer." In the same vein, you could offer to learn some new information related to the job responsibilities within your area, and in turn, pass on that information to the others that need to learn that same information.

*You could choose to become part of an outreach program, offered by your company, that occasionally presents seminars or classes to local high school or college students on topics related to workplace functions/behaviors. This could include information such as "workplace etiquette", "time management", "interview skills", "career choices", or other topics that are part of the school curriculum.

*You could make a decision to mentor future leaders through a national program titled SCORE, where former executives give of their time and talents to coach others who want to learn the "in's and out's" of business management.

*You could volunteer to give talks or presentations to local groups on topics related to your individual work or to the goals of your company. Local organizations, such as the Jaycees, Chambers of Commerce, Church Groups, etc. are always looking for speakers that can pique their interest. You could be that speaker.

The above are samplings of the many ways in which you can choose to share your business knowledge. And this type of formal or informal teaching can be accomplished either while employed or retired. In fact, many companies appreciate and allow their employees to become involved in outreach programs that will enhance the training of individuals. These opportunities not only are a source of public relations for the company, but more importantly, allow you the opportunity to become an "expert in a field", a chance for your own public relations to be born.

SELF TEST

*Does teaching in a formal university setting appeal to you?

*If so, what colleges are of interest? Who will you talk with?

*Are you willing to become a trainer within your own company?

*If so, whom will you approach regarding this idea?

*Do you wish to share your knowledge with the technical schools?

*If so, what knowledge do you wish to share?

*Do you wish to work with SCORE?

*Do you wish to become an "ambassador of your company, by presenting seminars or talks to local groups?

*If so, what topics would you like to present?

11

WHEN WILL YOU ACCOMPLISH YOUR PLAN

Congratulations

You have finished making your decisions about which route you wish to take as you move into the challenging 50's plus part of your life. Now comes the challenge to establish a realistic timeline to implement your decisions. You can plan that it may realistically take six months to set and accomplish the objectives of your decision/plan. Good luck with your future.

1. I INTEND TO ACCOMPLISH MY OVERALL DECISION/ PLAN BY (DATE).

2. STEPS I NEED TO TAKE TO ACCOMPLISH MY PLAN:

*STEP ONE:

DATE BY WHICH STEP ONE WILL BE ACCOMPLISHED.

*STEP TWO:

DATE BY WHICH STEP TWO WILL BE ACCOMPLISHED.

*STEP THREE:

DATE BY WHICH STEP THREE WILL BE ACCOMPLISHED.

*STEP FOUR:

DATE BY WHICH STEP FOUR WILL BE ACCOMPLISHED.

*STEP FIVE:

DATE BY WHICH STEP FIVE WILL BE ACCOMPLISHED.

APPENDIX

IDENTIFYING YOUR WORK VALUES

Many of you will remember a college theory, which was based on Maslow's Hierarchy of Needs. Maslow said that you work for three basic reasons: 1. Physical Needs (money, benefits, location, etc.) 2. Interactions with people (teamwork, colleagues, etc.) 3. Self Actualization (use of talents, contributions you can make, etc.) Depending on the situations in your life, you may move along and between the three different modes many times in your life.

Sometimes, it is a good idea to take some time to analyze why you want to work in the first place, and what is important in terms of your work values. This may be a good barometer on which to evaluate your decisions mentioned in the previous chapters.

EXPERTISE: Do you need to be recognized for your competence and proficiency in a specific field, or are you willing to be a part of the work experience but do not need recognition?

SCHEDULING: Do you prefer to have a set work schedule, so you can plan ahead, or do you prefer a schedule that is flexible and you can set your own timeframes?

ETHICS: Is it important that the workplace has principles that are consistent with your personal values?

RESPONSIBILITY: Do you need to "be in charge" or certain projects or people or do you prefer to have others responsible and accountable for the final result?

INCOME: How much money do you need to live comfortably, or how much money do you want to accrue for the future or for extra current "things"?

DECISION-MAKING: Do you want to have the ability to make final decisions, or do you prefer not have the responsibility?

PEOPLE CONTACT: Is it important to have people contact as part of your job, or do you prefer to work alone or behind the scenes?

SECURITY: How import is security for you, the need to know that you have a job that appears to be secure in terms of time, or are you able to live knowing that your job may be a short term experience?

BENEFITS: Is it important for you to have company benefits or do you have access to these types of compensation through other venues?

FUN: Do you look upon the workplace as a place you want to be as part of your entertainment life (in the broad sense), or do you believe that your job is just that/a chance to "make money", so you can do fun things outside of work?

CREATIVITY: Is your job an outlet to use your creative side/your chance to develop new ideas, etc. or do you prefer to have someone else develop the ideas?

MANAGEMENT: Do you wish to have a people management/leadership position or do you prefer not to be in charge?

CUTTING EDGE: Do you want to be with a company that is on the forefront of product/service areas or is this not important to you?

The above is a sampling of many of the work values that you may want to take some time to identify your principles. You may not be able to fulfill every work value, but it is important to utilize some of these areas as you make your decision about your future 50's/60's work/retirement life.

SELF TEST

Take a few moments to examine the important needs for you at this point in your life.

*ENVIRONMENT: (what is important to you in regard to physical surroundings)

*How large of a dwelling do you need?

*If you still need to make house payments, how much can you afford?

*What setting is important for your dwelling?

MONIES: (what are some of the financial decisions that you need to make for the future)

*What type of money do you need to live comfortably?

*Today?

*Next year?

*Five years from now?

*What will your insurance premiums be in the future?

*How much money can you expect from Social Security?

*How much income can you expect from severance? (if applicable)

*How much income can you expect from retirement savings?

LOCATION: (what aspects of geography will be applicable as part of your decisions)

*Is it important to remain near family and friends?

*Are you willing to pickup and start a new life either for a new job or for retirement?

RECREATION/SOCIAL: (what sort of hobbies, social groups, recreational activities do you want to continue)

*What types of activities are important to you?

*Are those activities connected with your work group?

*Are these activities connected with future retirement options?

FRIENDS: (are important are friends to you as you make future decisions)

*List all the friends that you need to consider as you make your 50"s Plus choice to work or not to work.

EHTICS/PRINCIPLES: (what types of underpinnings will be involved in future decisions)

*List the important spiritual/ethical considerations as you make future choices.

*Type and place of worship (if applicable)

*Discussion group centered around topics of values

*Moral ethics of a company

FAMILY: (is family a component part of your decision making)

*List all the family members impacted by your future decisions.

ABOUT THE AUTHOR

Mary Ann Peters is an expert career advisor who has been in the field of career management for the past 20 years, both on the corporate and individual level. Mary Ann has a Master's Degree in Human Resources from Webster University in St. Louis. She is certified as a Job and Career Transition Coach.

Mary Ann has been a regular contributor to the St. Louis Post Dispatch, where she has written series of articles on topics related to career growth. She also writes creative articles for the The Homesteader, a newspaper dedicated to new homeowners. She has also taught career seminars for the St. Louis Community College and for businesses in the St. Louis area.

Mary Ann currently resides in the metro St. Louis area. Her website is: www:thefiftiesplus.com.

978-0-595-38737-3
0-595-38737-3